GET PAID MORE
AND
PROMOTED FASTER

GET PAID
MORE
AND
PROMOTED
FASTER

BRIAN TRACY

BERRETT-KOEHLER PUBLISHERS, INC.
San Francisco

Berrett-Koehler Publishers, Inc.
235 Montgomery Street, Suite 650
San Francisco, CA 94104-2916
Tel: (415) 288-0260   Fax: (415) 362-2512   www.bkconnection.com

ORDERING INFORMATION

Quantity sales. Special discounts are available on quantity purchases by corporations, associations, and others. For details, contact the "Special Sales Department" at the Berrett-Koehler address above.

Individual sales. Berrett-Koehler publications are available through most bookstores. They can also be ordered direct from Berrett-Koehler: Tel: (800) 929-2929; Fax: (802) 864-7626; www.bkconnection.com

Orders for college textbook/course adoption use. Please contact Berrett-Koehler: Tel: (800) 929-2929; Fax: (802) 864-7626.

Orders by U.S. trade bookstores and wholesalers. Please contact Publishers Group West, 1700 Fourth Street, Berkeley, CA 94710. Tel: (510) 528-1444; Fax: (510) 528-3444.

Printed in the United States of America

Printed on acid-free and recycled paper that is composed of 50% recovered fiber, including 10% postconsumer waste.

Library of Congress Cataloging-in-Publication Data
Tracy, Brian.
    Get paid more and promoted faster : 21 great ways to get ahead in your career / Brian Tracy.
        p. cm.
    Includes index.
    ISBN 1-58376-207-8
    1. Career development.   2. Promotions.   I. Title.
HF5381.T65 2001
658.14—dc21   2001035708

Copyediting and proofreading by PeopleSpeak.
Book design and composition by Beverly Butterfield, Girl of the West Productions.

FIRST EDITION
05   04   03   02   01   10   9   8   7   6   5   4   3   2   1

This book is dedicated to my good friend and business partner, Victor Risling, a man who exemplifies the finest qualities of commitment, dedication, responsibility, and the willingness to always go the extra mile to get the job done. Victor is the ultimate role model for anyone who truly wants to get paid more and promoted faster.

Contents

Preface

This book is for anyone who wants to take full control over his or her career. If you feel that you are deserving of far more than you are receiving today, you are probably right. This book will show you how to get it. The twenty-one ideas you are about to learn will give you a series of practical, proven techniques that you can implement immediately to move upward and onward more rapidly in any company or job.

These strategies have been distilled and condensed from my more than thirty years of experience in the world of work, at every level, from the most menial job all the way up to the executive suite. I started as a dishwasher and then was a stock boy in a department store. I worked my way through more than twenty different jobs in varying industries and different countries, learning these principles the hard way as I struggled forward.

Throughout my career, I was continually looking around me and asking, "Why is it that some people are more successful than others?" Specifically, why do some people get paid more and promoted faster at work and others not?

Over the years, I rose from laboring jobs through sales and into management, eventually becoming the chief operating officer of a $265 million company. Today, I consult with the executives of some of the biggest companies in the world on the subjects of career development and personal success.

In my various positions, I have hired, trained, advised, appraised, promoted, and fired countless people, from junior staff up to company presidents. I have designed and conducted seminars for thousands of ambitious men and women who wanted to get ahead more rapidly.

In my advanced personal coaching programs, I work with successful executives and entrepreneurs to help them to strategize and reorganize themselves to do more of the right things, in the right way, so they can increase their incomes at a faster rate than ever before.

These ideas apply to you, whatever you are doing today. The fact is that you are probably worth twice as much as you are earning right now. You may be worth five or ten times as much. But it is completely up to you to take the necessary actions to maximize your potential at work.

You are in charge. You are the architect of your own career. You largely determine everything that happens to you, especially in the long term. Your chief responsibility to yourself in your work is to increase your ROE, your "return on energy." Your main goal should be to get the highest return on the part of your life that you invest in your job. Your aim should be to get paid the very most possible for the amount of time you spend.

It takes just as many years to be a big success in your field as to be average. And the truth is that you are not average. You probably have the capacity to be extraordinary in some way, and possibly in many ways. You almost certainly have within you, at this very moment, untapped talents and abilities that you have never fully utilized. Your job is to identify your special talents and then to apply them to getting the very most out of yourself and your career.

This book has one single focus: career success. It is not about balance, quality of life, or the importance of personal relationships. These vital subjects are better dealt with in another place.

The twenty-one great ideas in this book are aimed solely at helping you fulfill your desire to do as well as you possibly can in your chosen field. These principles are based on the fact that you are in charge of your own career and your own future. You are not a passive agent waiting and hoping for good things to happen to you. Rather, you are the primary creative force in your own life. You are a creator of circumstances, not simply a creature of circumstance.

Every idea, method, strategy, and technique you are about to learn has been tested and proven in the crucible of practical experience. Thousands of men and women are applying these principles every day to dramatically improve their results at work. Regular use of these "twenty-one great ways" will save you years of hard work in reaching the same level of income and success. And there are no real limits on what you can accomplish except for the limits you place on yourself.

BRIAN TRACY
Solana Beach, California
April 2001

GET PAID MORE
MORE
AND
PROMOTED
FASTER

Introduction:
Taking Charge of Your
Career and Your Future

This is a wonderful time in human history to be alive. There have never been more opportunities and possibilities for ambitious people to achieve their career and life goals than exist today.

Your responsibility to yourself and your world is to take full advantage of the doors opening all around you. Your duty is to participate with all your talents and abilities in what many economists are calling "the Golden Age of mankind." This book will show you how to do it.

In the coming pages, you will learn a series of practical, proven, simple, and effective ways to get paid more money for what you do. You will learn how to get promoted faster to higher levels of authority and responsibility. You will learn how to supercharge your career and put yourself onto the fast track at work.

These methods and techniques are used by the highest paid and most successful people in our society. When you begin to practice them yourself, you will put your foot onto the accelerator of your life and begin racing ahead in your career. You will make more progress in the next couple of years than the average person makes in ten or twenty years of just plodding along with the crowd.

We have moved from an era of lifelong employment to an era of lifelong employability. This means that from now on, you are completely responsible for every part of your work and personal life. One of the biggest mistakes you can ever make is to think that you work for anyone but yourself. No matter who signs your paycheck, you are always your own boss. You are always self-employed. In the long run, you determine how much you get paid, how fast you get promoted, and everything else that happens to you. You are responsible.

The top 3 percent of Americans in terms of pay and promotion view themselves as self-employed, no matter where they work or whom they work for. This attitude of self-employment, of taking complete responsibility for results, makes them more valuable to their companies and to themselves. As a result, more doors open for them. They get paid more and promoted faster.

From now on, see yourself as the president of a company with one employee—yourself. See yourself as responsible for selling one product into a competitive marketplace—your personal services. See yourself as a consultant to your existing company who is determined to justify the amount you are paid every hour of every day.

Then, begin implementing the twenty-one great ways to get paid more and promoted faster that all fast-trackers use to move ahead more rapidly in their careers. You will never look back.

Decide Exactly What You Want

The world has a habit of making room
for the man whose words and actions
show that he knows where he is going.

—NAPOLEON HILL

This is the "giant step" in personal success and achievement. Decide what you really want from your career. Take the time to analyze your personal talents and abilities. Look deep into yourself to determine what you really enjoy doing. Identify the tasks and activities that most interest you and hold your attention. Think back over your past jobs. What have been your most satisfying experiences and your most enjoyable moments?

You are nature's greatest miracle. You are the end result of millions of years of evolution. There never has been, nor ever will be, anyone exactly like you. In your genetic code, you have been programmed with remarkable potential abilities that you can develop to perform certain tasks extraordinarily well.

You have been engineered for success from birth. You have within you deep reservoirs of talent and potential skill that you have not yet tapped into. You have the capacity to be, do, and have virtually anything that you put your mind to. But you must first accept the responsibility of deciding exactly what you really want and then dedicate yourself wholeheartedly to becoming everything you are capable of becoming.

In deciding what you really want, practice the process of *idealization* in your career. Project yourself forward five years and imagine that you were doing the ideal job, with the ideal people, at the ideal salary, and under the ideal conditions. What would it look like? Define your ideal clearly and then determine what you would have to do, starting today, to make it a reality.

Imagine for a moment that you could have any job at all. Imagine that all jobs and positions are open to you. Imagine that there is a job that you would really enjoy doing, hour after hour and day after day.

One of the greatest of all success secrets is for you to decide what you really enjoy doing and then find a way to make a good living doing just that. And this is up to you. No one else can do it for you. You are responsible.

You will almost always be paid more and promoted faster when you are doing something that you enjoy, something that you find interesting and challenging and that stimulates and motivates you. The fact is that unless you really enjoy your work, you will never be able to develop the commitment, enthusiasm, and dedication necessary to rise above and push through the difficulties, challenges, and setbacks that every job or career contains.

To clarify your thinking, practice *zero-based thinking* regularly in your career and in your personal life. This method of analysis is a key thinking skill that comes from zero-based accounting and is one of the most powerful thinking techniques that you can learn and practice.

The way it works is simple. In zero-based accounting, you look at every expense and ask, "If we were not now engaged in this expenditure, knowing what we now know, would we begin it again today?"

Zero-based thinking is similar. Consider all of your previous decisions and ask yourself this question: "Is there anything in my life that I am doing today that, knowing what I now know, I wouldn't get into again today if I had to do it over?"

This is one of the most helpful questions you can ever ask and answer. *Is there anything in your life that you are doing today that, knowing what you now know, you wouldn't get into again today if you had to do it over?*

The fact is that in times of turbulence and rapid change such as today, and probably for the rest of your career, you will always be able to say yes to that question regarding some area of your life or work.

Apply zero-based thinking to your current job. Knowing what you now know, would you take this job again on the same terms and conditions that you are now working under? Would you take this job working for this particular boss? Would you go to work for this company? In this industry? At this salary? Or in this position? Yes or no?

If the answer is no, your next question is, "How do I change this situation, and how fast can I do it?" You are responsible.

You may have to invest a lot of effort and make a lot of false starts before your ideal career. But it all begins with your sitting down and deciding what you really want in a job, as well as what you don't want, and then taking action to achieve that goal.

TAKE ACTION NOW!

Make up a "dream list" for your ideal job or position. Begin by imagining that you have no limitations on what you could do. Imagine that all possibilities are open to you. Imagine that you have all the education, all the knowledge, all the experience, all the contacts, and all the time and money you need. What job would you choose if you could have any job at all?

Think in terms of specific actions that you could take immediately. What could you do right now to begin preparing yourself and moving toward the exact job or position you really want? Whatever your answer, do something, do anything, but get started. You are responsible.

Select the Right Company

The choice is yours. You hold the tiller.

You can steer the course you choose

in the direction of where you want

to be—today, tomorrow, or in a

distant time to come.

—W. CLEMENT STONE

In these times of continuous and accelerating change, some industries are growing and expanding and absorbing many thousands of people. These industries are offering incredible opportunities for men and women who want to get ahead faster than the average person.

In the meantime, many other industries have leveled off or are actually declining in economic importance and employment. These industries continue to hire people to replace the workers who quit or retire, but as a result of automation, new technology, changing consumer preferences, and competition, these industries are not likely to grow much in the years ahead. Your first job in the pursuit of great career success is to separate the high-growth industries from the low-growth industries.

You can make more progress toward getting paid more and promoted faster in a high-growth industry in a couple of years than you might in five or ten years in a slow-growth industry. Many people change their entire lives by simply walking across the street and taking a different job in a different company in a faster growing sector of the economy.

Look upon your special combination of talents and abilities as a precious resource, like money, and view the job market as a place where you are going to invest yourself to get the very highest return. Treat your mental, emotional, and physical energies as your "human capital," to be allocated in such a way as to give you the maximum payoff. Be perfectly selfish when it comes to committing your life and your work to a particular company or a particular industry.

When you find the right job in the right company, you should then throw your whole heart into doing that job in an excellent fashion. Continually look for ways to increase your value. This strategy will put you in a perfect position to be paid more and promoted faster in the months and years ahead.

TAKE ACTION NOW!

Look around you in the marketplace of jobs and careers today. Identify the companies and industries that are getting the most attention in the news because of their new products, processes, and growth rates. Decide if any company or industry out there interests you, attracts you, draws you toward it.

Do your research. Check newspapers, magazines, and libraries. Surf the Internet. The power is on the side of the person with the best information. Then, start talking to people who work with or in the type of companies you are attracted to. Apply for a position and ask what skills or competencies a person would need to succeed in that business. This research process could change your whole life.

Choose the Right Boss

The greatest power that a person possesses is the power to choose.

—J. Martin Kohe

Your choice of the right boss can help your career and assure that you get paid more and promoted faster more than almost anything else you can do.

Taking a job is similar to entering into a business marriage, with your boss as your "business spouse." He or she is going to have an enormous impact on how much you get paid, how much you enjoy your work, how rapidly you get promoted, and every other part of your work life.

When you are looking for a job, you should ask your potential boss a lot of questions. Make sure that this is the kind of person that you would enjoy working with and for. Be sure that this is someone whom you could like, respect, and look up to. You should be convinced that this is someone who is friendly and supportive and a person you can rely on to help you move ahead as rapidly as possible in your career.

The very best bosses seem to have certain common qualities, no matter what the business or industry. First of all, good bosses have high integrity. When they make a promise, they keep it. When they say they will do something, they do it exactly as they said they would. If they promise you a salary review or an increase, they follow through, right on schedule.

The best bosses are very clear when they describe a task to you. They take the time to make sure you understand exactly what you are expected to do and to what standard and by what deadline. They ask for your ideas and your input and are always open to new and better ways to get the job done.

The best bosses are considerate and caring about their employees. This means that they are interested in you as a person as well as an employee. They take an interest in your personal life and your family. They want to know about the things that concern you and that affect the way you think and feel at work.

This doesn't mean that a good boss is a father or mother confessor or a nursemaid. But a good boss sees you as a whole person with a life apart from your work life.

You can always tell the quality of your relationship with your boss by measuring how free you feel to speak honestly, openly, and directly to him or her about matters that concern you. When you see your boss coming, you should feel confident and happy rather than nervous or insecure.

Perhaps the best measure of all is that when you are working with the right boss, at the right job, you feel happy and relaxed. You laugh a lot at work. You enjoy yourself and you feel valuable and important as an employee and as a person.

Working for a great boss is a good way to get paid more and promoted faster. And there are lots of great bosses out there.

◆

TAKE ACTION NOW!

Imagine your perfect boss today. Think about the best bosses or teachers you have had in the past. Identify the qualities and behaviors they had in common. How does your picture of an ideal boss compare with your current boss?

Take the initiative to improve your relationship with your boss if you feel it is necessary. Go to your boss and tell him or her honestly and directly what he or she could do, or stop doing, to enable you to be more effective. Tell your boss what would help you to be happier and make a better contribution to the company. Most bosses are very open to this kind of positive feedback, as long as it is given in the spirit of helpfulness rather than as an attack or criticism.

Develop a
Positive Attitude

Every man is where he is by the law of his

being; the thoughts he has built into

his character have brought him there.

—JAMES ALLEN

Fully 85 percent of your success in work, according to psychologist Sydney Jourard, is determined by your attitude and your personality. Your progress, how much you are paid and how fast you are promoted, is largely determined by how much people like you and want to help you.

People who are cheerful and optimistic are always more liked and respected than those who are complaining and critical. One of the most important determinants of your success in your career is how well you get along with others and how well you perform as a part of a team. Your pay and promotion will be greatly influenced by how well you cooperate with others at every stage of your career.

The very best team players seem to be those who are pleasant, positive, and supportive of their coworkers. They have high levels of empathy and consideration. They are the kind of people that others want to be around, work with, and help to get ahead.

A positive, friendly person is more readily noticed and appreciated by superiors who can boost his or her career. In addition, a positive person receives more support from coworkers and staff. A more positive person experiences an upward pressure that pushes him or her forward at a faster rate.

The critical measure of how positive you really are is demonstrated by how you perform under stress. Anyone can be positive when things are going well. But it is when you face difficulties and setbacks that you demonstrate to yourself, and everyone around you, what you are truly made of. You've heard it said that "When the going gets tough, the tough get going."

A person with a positive mental attitude tries to look for the good in every person and every situation. He or she looks for something positive or constructive, or for a valuable lesson, in every problem. The habit of looking into every setback or difficulty for something worthwhile keeps you optimistic and cheerful. It keeps you future oriented and action oriented rather than backward or blame oriented.

Fortunately, this constructive approach is a habit you can develop with practice. A positive mental attitude is something that you learn by resolving to be positive every single day, especially when it is most needed.

◆ ─────────────────────────────

TAKE ACTION NOW!

Decide today that you are going to become a completely positive person at work and in your personal life. Refuse to criticize, complain, or condemn when things aren't going well. Resist the tendency to find fault, gossip, or gripe about other people or about any aspect of your company.

Resolve today to go on a "Twenty-One-Day Positive Mental Attitude Diet" at work. During this time, practice being completely positive and constructive all day long, no matter what happens. Count to ten before you react or respond to a problem or difficulty. Look for something good to say in every situation.

At the end of twenty-one days, you will have created a new habit that will serve you for the rest of your life.

Create a Successful Image

Most people are highly visual;
they therefore judge you by the way
you look on the outside, the same
way you judge them.

—Brian Tracy

Look the part! If you want to be a big success, to be accepted and respected by others, you must look like the kind of person others can admire and relate to.

It is absolutely amazing how many people hold themselves back, year after year, because of their ignorance or inattention to their external appearance. No one has ever taken them aside and told them how important their dress and grooming are to getting paid more and promoted faster.

Numerous articles and books have been written on the subject of professional image in business. I have personally studied the subject for years and taught image and dress to thousands of men and women. I have seen countless situations where a small change in someone's personal appearance has made all the difference in getting hired or promoted. How you look on the outside has a major effect on how far you go and how fast you get there.

People judge you, at least initially, by the way you look on the outside. You never get a second chance to make a good first impression. Your external appearance, your clothes, and your grooming determine 95 percent of the first impression you make. And these elements are determined solely by yourself.

Whether you know it or not, when you choose the clothes you are going to wear and how you groom yourself, you make a personal statement to the world. You tell others what you think of yourself, and you signal to others how they are to evaluate you and treat you. Since you dress yourself, you are responsible for whatever message you send.

Communication experts say that people judge you in the first four seconds and finalize their opinion of you in the next thirty seconds. What kind of an impression are you making when people meet you for the first time? What kind of an impression would you ideally like to make? What changes could you make to project a better first impression?

You should always "dress for success" at your job and in your company, however that is defined by your business or industry. To determine what constitutes successful dress, start by looking at the top people in your company. Look in newspapers and magazines at the pictures of the men and women who are being promoted to positions of higher responsibility and greater pay in your industry. Pattern yourself after these people—the leaders, not the followers.

The rule is that you should always dress for the position two positions above your current job. When you start to look like a person in a higher position, the people who determine your future at work begin to think of you performing at a higher level. They begin to think of you in terms of greater promotability.

Specific colors and color combinations are more effective than others in business. In addition, specific clothes and accessories convey a message of authority and competence. These vary from industry to industry and from company to company.

You should buy a good book on professional image, such as *Dress for Success* (for men and women) by John Molloy, read it from cover to cover, and then follow its recommendations in every element of your appearance. Leave nothing to chance.

> Rule: "If you are a person with a future,
> don't dress like a person without one."

There is a lot of talk today about casual dress and how the accepted norms for dress in business have changed. Much of this is only partially true or not true at all. Even the most indifferently dressed Silicon Valley dot-com executive keeps a suit handy to slip on when a client or a banker comes to visit.

Casual dress is appropriate only for employees who have limited customer contact and for people who have only an indirect influence on the fortunes of the company. In many companies, allowing the inside staff to dress down is used as a substitute for additional pay and promotion. You must be careful and thoughtful in this area as it applies to yourself. Follow the leaders, not the followers.

Dress like a person who is going somewhere in life. If everyone around you is dressing casually and you decide to dress well instead, who do you think is going to stand out and look even more like a serious person with a great future?

Senior executives want to be proud of the employees whom they introduce to their customers and other people. When you take special care to dress well, you look more competent and capable to those people who can help you in your career. You should dress and groom yourself like the kind of person that an executive would be happy to present to another executive as being a representative of your company.

Always strive to look like a winner at work. Act as if you are a valuable and important person. Create the appearance of a person with a great future who is going somewhere with this company. No matter what anyone says, human beings are strongly influenced by the external appearance and dress of other people. Your goal is to present yourself so that you look competent and confident in every business situation.

Never forget that you are a remarkable person with an unlimited future in front of you. It is important that everyone who sees you recognizes this fact when they meet you for the first time, and every time they see you thereafter.

TAKE ACTION NOW!

Resolve today that you are going to dress, groom, and look in every way as if you were already the big success you intend to be. Look around you at the most successful people in your company and pattern yourself after them. Ignore the people who dress down and instead dress every day as if you were going for a job interview later in the afternoon.

Go out today, or go to the Internet, and buy at least one good book on clothes, styles, fabrics, and grooming. Learn how to combine colors and accessories. Examine your current wardrobe and get rid of those clothes that are no longer consistent with the message you want to send.

Start Earlier, Work Harder, and Stay Later

The end of life is life. Life is action,
the use of one's powers, and to use them
to their height is our joy and duty.

—ANONYMOUS

Develop a commitment to hard work. Nothing will bring you to the attention of the important people in your work life faster than for you to get a reputation as a person who works hard and gets a lot done.

A hard worker is not an antisocial personality or a driven, compulsive personality who burns out from stress and overwork. Rather, a hard worker is a person who does not waste time. He or she makes every minute count at work. He or she sets clear priorities, works steadily throughout the day, and is determined to make a valuable contribution to the company.

Everybody knows who the hardest workers are in every organization. They are always the ones who are the most respected in a company. They are almost always paid more and promoted faster—and for very good reasons. They get more work done in a shorter period of time. They make a greater contribution per each dollar that they receive in pay. As a result, they are more valuable to the company. They are a better investment. They set a better example and they are the kind of people that bosses are proud of and want to hold onto more than anyone else.

Two extra hours of productive work each day is all you really need to invest to become one of the most valuable and effective people in your company. You can create this extra two hours by coming in an hour earlier and staying one hour later. This will expand your day slightly, but it will accelerate your career tremendously.

Efficiency experts have determined that you get the equivalent of three hours of office work done for every one hour that you work without interruptions. The truth is that because of interruptions and distractions, you get very little work, especially creative work, done in the office. You must be continually carving out blocks of time where you can work nonstop. You can get this extra time by coming in before anyone else, working while others are out at lunch, and staying a little later, after the others have left for the day.

The top people in every field work more hours than the average person. The top 10 percent of money earners in America work fifty hours or more per week. The highest paid 1 percent of Americans work an average of fifty-six hours per week. And more importantly, they work all the time they work. They do not waste time. They arrive at work early and they immediately start on their most important tasks. They work steadily throughout the day. They are friendly, but they do not spend the day making small talk or engaging in idle chitchat with their coworkers.

This must be your goal as well. Work all the time you are at work. Do not drop off your dry cleaning, make personal phone calls, read the newspaper, or chat about the latest football game or television program. Work all the time you work.

Imagine that your company is going to bring in an outside firm to analyze everyone in terms of who works the hardest, who works the second hardest, and all the way down to who works the least. Your goal is to win this imaginary contest. Your job is to be ranked as the hardest working person in the entire company. Winning this imaginary competition will help you to get paid more and promoted faster than almost any other reputation you could possibly develop. And this competition is going on every day, whether anyone has told you about it or not.

When a coworker wants to chat or tries to distract you from what you are doing, be polite but firm. Tell him or her that you are really busy right now. Offer to get together later. Then, smile cheerfully and say, "Well, I've got to get back to work!"

Keep repeating these words, over and over, "Back to work! Back to work! Back to work!"

These words, continually repeated, will motivate you to overcome procrastination, stay focused on your key tasks, and become one of the most productive people in your business. And everyone will notice.

◆

TAKE ACTION NOW!

Resolve today that you are going to become the hardest working person at your company. Reorganize your schedule so that you come in one hour before anyone else and get started immediately. Don't tell anyone else what you are doing. The people who matter the most to you will notice soon enough.

Work all the time you are at work. Cut back on coffee breaks and lunches where you waste time in idle chatter. Instead, use that time to get more done. Stay an hour later to get ahead of your work. In no time, you will be producing two and three times as much work as the other people around you.

Push to
the Front

Man was created as a being who should
constantly keep improving, a being who
on reaching one goal sets a higher one.

—RALPH RANSOM

The fact is that all of life is a contest of some kind. You are in competition with everyone else who wants to be paid more and promoted faster, whether you like it or not. A race is on and you are in it. Your job is to move yourself into the lead and then figure out how to move ahead faster than the other people around you.

Fortunately, there are proven and tested ways to get ahead and stay ahead. One of the most important of these strategies is for you to continually ask for more responsibility. Volunteer for every assignment. Go to your boss at least once every week and ask him or her if there is something more that you can do.

At staff meetings, people are always making suggestions about things that should or could be done to solve problems or achieve company goals faster. Whenever you see your boss buying in to one of these ideas, you should volunteer for the additional task. Raise your hand. Grab the new job as a football player would grab a fumble and run for yardage. Then, do the job quickly.

Most people in the world of work have never thought of this simple strategy. They do only what is asked of them, when it is asked of them. They even think it is clever to get by doing the very least possible. But you do the opposite. You keep asking for more tasks and responsibilities. You then move to complete these tasks quickly and dependably.

Don't worry about being taken advantage of. By asking for more and more responsibility, you are actually taking advantage of your company and your boss. You are expanding and increasing your knowledge and skill, your ability to get results. You are building a better and better reputation for contributing value to your organization. This will always benefit you, both in the short term and throughout your career.

Few strategies are better for helping you to get paid more and promoted faster than for you to develop a reputation for offering to do more than anyone else. Whatever extra effort or sacrifice you have to make, treat every assignment that you receive as if it were a test upon which your future career depended, and then go to work to complete it quickly and well.

◆

TAKE ACTION NOW!

Continually look for ways to make yourself more valuable, especially by volunteering for tasks that are important to your boss. Go to your boss regularly and ask if there is anything that you can take off his or her shoulders, anything that he or she needs doing. You'll be amazed at the opportunities you will get to increase your value.

Offer to help whenever something needs to be done. Volunteer for assignments and additional work. Because no one else does this, you'll stand out almost immediately. Then, whatever the task, do it quickly, report back to your boss, and ask for more responsibility.

Ask for What You Want

The people who get on in this world
are the people who get up and look for
the circumstances they want, and,
if they can't find them, make them.

—George Bernard Shaw

Asking for what you want is one of the success principles. It is one of the most important actions you can take to get paid more than you are getting today. The future belongs to the askers. The future does not belong to those people who sit back, wishing and hoping that things will improve. The future belongs to those people who step up and ask for what they want. And if they don't get it right away, they ask, again and again, until they do get it.

Ask your boss what you have to do to qualify for an increase in pay. There is no point in your working very hard if you do not know exactly what you have

to do to get ahead. Clarity is essential. Go to your boss
and ask, and ask again if you are still not clear.

If you want more money, you must ask for it. It is
not going to fall on you out of the sky. The best way
to ask is by building a case, as a lawyer would build a
case, for the amount that you want to receive. Put
your case in writing, like a business proposal. Instead
of saying that you need more money, as most people
do, your strategy should be different. You should put
together a list of the jobs that you are doing and the
additional experience and skills you have developed
since your last increase. You should explain the financial impact of your work on the overall operations
of the company and the contribution that you are
making as a top employee.

You should then present all this information exactly as if you were making a sales presentation to
your boss and tell him or her that, based on your
proof of performance, you would like an increase of a
specific amount of money per month or per year. In
many cases, you will get the increase simply by asking for it in an intelligent way. In some cases, you will
get less than you requested. If this happens, ask what
you will have to do in the future to get the rest of the
increase that you have asked for. How can you make
yourself more valuable?

Treat your request for an increase as if it were an
important negotiation, with long-term consequences,

because it is. Arrange a meeting with your boss in advance. Be sure the timing is convenient and that you aren't rushed. Sometimes such a meeting is best scheduled at the end of the day, when everything has settled down and there are no interruptions. Be relaxed, calm, and positive. Then ask for what you want with confidence, courage, and an attitude of positive expectancy.

If your request for an increase is turned down completely, remain calm and positive. Ask exactly what you will have to do in the future to get the increase you requested, and exactly when that increase will be payable. Be specific. Be clear. And don't be afraid to ask.

Of course, you should ask politely. Ask courteously. Ask in a warm and friendly way. Ask cheerfully. Ask expectantly. Ask confidently. And ask persistently, if necessary. But be sure to ask. The future belongs to the people who continually ask for what they want, in every area of life. The more you ask for the things you want, the more likely you are to get them. Try this asking strategy at every opportunity and you will be amazed at the good things that happen to you.

◆

TAKE ACTION NOW!

Do your homework. Find out what you are really worth in terms of the contribution you are making and the amounts being paid to similar people doing similar jobs both within your company and in other companies. Call employee placement companies and ask them what someone like you would be worth on the open market. Look at what is being offered for similar jobs in newspaper ads.

Show your boss clearly, on paper, the value that you are contributing in terms of added revenues, decreased costs, increased output, or greater efficiencies. Explain how your higher level of experience or additional training makes you a more valuable employee. Compare your current income with what the company would have to pay to hire and train someone else to do the same job. Be specific about the amount you want. And then ask.

Guard Your Integrity as a Sacred Thing

Every germ of goodness will at last

struggle into bloom and fruitage;

true success follows every right step.

—Orison Swett Marden

All successful business is based on trust. All relationships with customers, suppliers, employees, and financial institutions are based on knowing that people can trust you to do what you say you will. Theodore Leavitt, dean of the Harvard Business School, says, "The most valuable asset a company has is its reputation, the way it is known to its customers."

In the same way, your character and reputation are perhaps your most valuable assets in your career. Your reputation for integrity and honest dealing is the critical factor that others use to judge you when they evaluate you for higher pay or for a position of greater responsibility.

The first key element of character is truthfulness with others. No matter what, always tell the truth in every situation. When you give your word, keep it. When you make a promise, fulfill it. When you say you'll do something, no matter what the inconvenience or difficulty, be sure to do it.

The second element of character is dependability. Few qualities are so important, valued, and respected in business, and in life, as the dependability of a person who says he or she will do something or be somewhere. It is worth any sacrifice or inconvenience for you to deliver on your promises. It is essential for you to be the kind of person that others can rely on completely.

The third element of character is loyalty. Lack of loyalty is one of the major reasons for failure and underachievement in business and in life. When you are truly loyal, you do not complain to others about your company or your boss. Instead, if you are unhappy or dissatisfied for any reason, you address your concern in a direct and straightforward way. You go to the person involved and deal with the issue. You take responsibility and take action.

You do not condemn or criticize your company, your boss, your products or services, or anything else about your work to the outside world. If you are not willing to do something about it, you keep it to yourself. You always support the people you work with and for. You demonstrate and express complete loyalty to the person who signs your paycheck. If you cannot do this for any reason, you should go somewhere else where you can.

William Shakespeare once wrote, "To thine own self be true, and it must follow, as the night the day, thou canst not then be false to any man."

You remain true to yourself by listening to your inner voice and trusting your conscience. Then, be true to everyone around you. Always live in truth by saying and doing only what you know to be honest and sincere. Never compromise your integrity for anything.

The good news is that when you live with complete integrity, inside and outside, you feel wonderful about yourself. You have greater self-confidence and higher self-esteem. You feel positive and powerful. And most of all, you earn the respect, trust, and loyalty of all the important people around you. Always guard your integrity as a sacred thing.

◆

TAKE ACTION NOW!

Do what you say you will do, when you say you will do it, whether you feel like it or not, or whether it is convenient or not. Develop a reputation for absolute trustworthiness in every area of your personal and business life.

Resolve to be correct and dependable in matters of time and scheduling. Be punctual for meetings. Complete assignments on time, as promised. If for any reason you cannot make a deadline, be sure that others know well in advance.

Think about the Future

Visualize this thing that you want. See it, feel it, and believe in it. Make your mental blueprint and then begin to build.

—Maxwell Maltz

Perhaps the greatest insight into human behavior and individual destiny is that "You become what you think about most of the time."

Your predominant thoughts largely determine what you say, how you decide and act, the results you get, and the entire course of your life. You always tend to move in the direction of your dominant dreams and aspirations. The more you think, talk, and imagine something, the more of an impact it has on your feelings and actions, and the more rapidly you attract it into your life.

Successful people, in every walk of life, think and talk about what they want most of the time. They think and talk about the future and how they can make it a reality. They are continually thinking and talking about where they are going and how to get there the very fastest way possible. As a result, they continually see possibilities and have insights that enable them to move more rapidly toward their goals.

Developing the habit of future orientation requires that you create a long-term vision for yourself and for your career. This habit of thinking about where you are going and where you want to end up will have an enormous impact on your level of success.

Dr. Edward Banfield of Harvard University, after more than fifty years of research, concluded that the most successful men and women in our society are those who have a "long time perspective." They think ten and twenty years out into the future, and they make their decisions each day based on this long time horizon. So should you.

The most important word in future orientation, as we talked about in chapter 1, is "idealization." The process of idealization, in this sense, requires that you continually think about and imagine your ideal future career. Regularly project yourself forward three to five years. Imagine that your career were perfect in every respect and that you were doing exactly the right job for you.

If your job were ideal in every respect, what would it look like? What sort of work would you be doing? How much would you be earning? Who would you be working with? Where would you be working?

What level of responsibility would you have? Allow this picture to influence and guide your day-to-day decisions.

Once you have imagined and idealized your perfect job, visualize the kind of person you would have to become in order to get and keep that job. What kind of skills would you have? What new skills and core competencies would you have to develop?

Practice what is called "gap analysis" on your job. Look at the difference between where you are today and where you would like to be in the future. Identify the gap that exists between the two situations. What is the biggest single difference?

What changes should you begin making, right now, to bridge that gap? What steps could you take today to begin taking full control over your destiny and to prepare yourself for the kind of job you really want? As management guru Peter Drucker said, "The very best way to predict the future is to create it."

The more you develop a clear vision of where you want to be in the years ahead, the more likely it is that you will take those steps, each day, that will translate your vision into reality.

Think about the future of your company as well. Think about where your company is going and what your company needs to accomplish to be successful and profitable in the future. Think about what you could do personally to help your company get to where it wants to go.

The more future oriented you are in your position, the greater contribution you are likely to make. The more you contribute to achieving the company's long-term goals, the more you will be paid and the more rapidly you will be promoted. The more future oriented you are, the better decisions you will make and the more positive impact you will have on your company's operations. The more future oriented you are, the more you will feel in control of your life, your career, and your personal destiny.

◆

TAKE ACTION NOW!

Take out a sheet of paper and write down as many details as possible that would describe your perfect job, life, and career sometime in the distant future. Let your imagination float freely. Imagine that a billionaire is going to take this list from you and give you the exact job you describe. Define it clearly.

Look around you at what you are doing today. Compare your current situation, your current level of knowledge and skills, with what you would ideally like to be doing sometime in the future. Whatever changes you would have to make to create your perfect future, begin making those changes today.

Focus on Your Goals

People with goals succeed because
they know where they're going.

—Earl Nightingale

Perhaps the most important single word in achieving great success in your work and personal life is the word "clarity." Clarity requires that you become absolutely clear about who you are, what you believe, what you are (or could be) really good at, and the goals you want to accomplish.

People who have clear, written goals and who know exactly what they want to accomplish in each area of their lives achieve vastly more than people who are unsure or unclear about what they want. In business, says Michael Eisner, CEO of the Walt Disney Company, "the person with the strongest point of view usually wins the day."

Perhaps nothing can help you to be paid more and promoted faster than for you to become an intensely goal-oriented person. Your ability to set and achieve goals is often called the "master skill" of success. Fortunately, all business skills are learnable, and this is one that you can learn quite quickly and then improve through practice, day after day.

There are many approaches to goal setting. You can even attend multiday seminars on the subject. The great truth, however, is that any method is better than no method at all. Here is a simple yet powerful seven-step formula you can use to set and achieve any goal.

◆ **Step one: Decide exactly what you want.**

Decide what you want to achieve in your career. Decide your ideal income, your desired lifestyle, your perfect family situation, your level of health, your weight and level of physical fitness, and your goals in every other area that is important to you. Most people never do this. When you know exactly what you want, you separate yourself from the majority of the population.

◆ **Step two: Write it down.**

When you write your goals down on paper, something amazing happens between your head and your hand. The act of writing actually programs these goals into your subconscious mind. They then begin to take on a power of their own, attracting people and possibilities into your life. Every person I have ever spoken with who began writing their goals down on a regular basis was absolutely amazed at how rapidly those goals were achieved.

- **Step three: Set a deadline.**

If it is a large goal, set subdeadlines as well. If you miss your deadline for any reason, set another deadline. Your subconscious mind needs a clear "forcing system" or specific time target to aim at. When you set a deadline, you activate more of your subconscious powers. You will feel yourself internally motivated to take those actions that are necessary to achieve your goal on schedule.

- **Step four: Make a list.**

Write down every task you can think of that you will have to complete to achieve your goal. As you think of new tasks and activities, add them to your list. Keep developing your list until it is complete. This is very important.

- **Step five: Organize your list into a plan.**

A plan is merely a list of activities arranged by time and sequence. What has to be done first? What can be done later? What is more important? What is less important? Once you have a goal and a plan, you will have a blueprint for success. You will be ready to achieve your goals at a more rapid rate than ever before.

♦ **Step six: Take action on your plan.**

Do something. Do anything. But whatever you do, get busy. Get going. Don't delay. Select the most logical first step and get started. It is amazing how many great goals and plans die for lack of implementation. Don't let this happen to you.

♦ **Step seven: Do something every day that moves you toward your major goal.**

Take specific actions that move you in the direction of your most important goal. This is perhaps the most important step of all. By doing something every day, you develop the power of momentum. With this power, you will move faster and faster toward your goal. At the same time, your goal will move faster and faster toward you.

The more goal oriented you are at work, the more focused you will be. The more focused you are, the less time you will waste and the more you will accomplish. The more you accomplish, the more valuable you will be to your company.

When you become intensely goal oriented, you will stand out from the other people around you. You will attract more opportunities for greater responsibilities. By becoming intensely goal oriented, you will inevitably get paid more and promoted faster.

TAKE ACTION NOW!

Take out a piece of paper right now and write down ten goals you would like to achieve in the next twelve months. Write these goals in the present tense ("I earn $XXX per year") exactly as if a year has passed and your goals have already been achieved.

Select the one goal from your list that could have the greatest positive impact on your life and career. Transfer this goal to a clean sheet of paper. Set a deadline on it. Make a written plan to achieve it. Take action on your plan and then resolve to do something every day to move you toward your goal. This powerful goal-setting exercise alone can change your life.

Concentrate on Results

The first requisite of success is the
ability to apply your physical and
mental energies to one problem or goal
incessantly without growing weary.

—Thomas Edison

Your ability to get results is the most important single determinant of how much you are paid and how rapidly you are promoted. Results are everything in the world of work. In study after study, researchers have found that within two years of leaving college or school, your education has little or no impact on your career. From that point on, all that really matters is your ability to perform and get results for your company.

Many people start off with limited education and skills, but as the result of focusing on results single-mindedly, they accomplish vastly more than people who begin with better educations and greater natural advantages. This must be your strategy as well.

To become more result oriented, ask yourself these three questions, all day long:

1. What are my highest value activities?

What are the things that you do that contribute the very most value to your work and to your company? This is where you should focus most of your time and energy. If you are not sure of the answer to this question, ask your boss.

2. What can I and only I do that, if done well, will make a real difference to my company?

This is one of the best questions you can ask and answer for ensuring intense result orientation. Your answer to this question will be a job or task that only you can do. If you do not do it, it will not get done. No one else can or will do it for you. Whatever your answer to this question, start to work on that specific task immediately.

3. What is the most valuable use of my time right now?

Every minute of every hour of every day, you should be working on the one activity that represents the most valuable use of your time at that moment. This will do more to increase your productivity, performance, and output than any other activity. Finishing this one task will enable you to contribute greater value than any other single job you could do at that moment.

The best days of your working life will be when you are working on those tasks that your boss considers to be the most important and valuable use of your time. There is no better way to get paid more and promoted faster than for you to be working, all day long, on the tasks that are of greatest concern to your boss.

The good news is that the more consistently you accomplish your most important tasks, the greater number of important tasks you will be given to accomplish. The more you produce results, the greater will be the results that will be entrusted to you. The more you contribute, the more you will be paid and the faster you will be promoted.

◆

TAKE ACTION NOW!

Why are you on the payroll? Make a list of everything you have been hired to do. Be sure to differentiate between activities and accomplishments, between inputs and the required outputs of your job. Then organize your list by priority, by what is most important and what is less important.

Take this list to your boss. Ask him or her to organize your tasks in order of his or her priorities. What does your boss consider to be the most important things you do, your highest value activities?

Whatever his or her answer, from this moment forward, resolve to work every day, every hour, on precisely those tasks that your boss has ranked as your highest value-added activities. This will propel you onto the fast track in your career as much or more than anything else you can do.

Be a Problem Solver

The power which resides in man is new in nature and none but he knows what that is which he can do, nor does he know until he has tried.

—RALPH WALDO EMERSON

Problems are a normal, natural, and unavoidable fact of life. Your work will be a continuous succession of problems, like the waves coming in from the ocean, one after another. You will have problem after problem all day long and into the evening. They never end. They only vary in size and importance.

The only part of this situation that you can control is your attitude, the way in which you approach each problem as it arises. Unfortunately, most people allow themselves to be overwhelmed by problems. They think and talk continually about who is to blame, why the problem occurred, and the possible damage or cost. But this is not helpful. Instead, your job is to be solution oriented and concentrate all your energies on what can be done to solve the problem, whatever it is.

Solution-oriented people are the most valuable people in any organization. They are positive and constructive. They concentrate on what can be done now rather than on what has already occurred and cannot be changed.

Here is a powerful principle. You can change your attitude from negative and worried to positive and constructive in a single moment by simply switching your thoughts off of the problem and onto the solution. Instead of asking or worrying about who did what and who is to blame, you should instead ask the questions, "What do we do now?" and "What's the solution?"

Your mind is designed in such a way that the more you focus on finding solutions, the more solutions you will find. The more you think and talk about solutions, the faster and easier you will come up with even better solutions. You will actually become more creative and competent at solving problems, dealing with difficulties, achieving goals, and getting key results as you discipline yourself to focus more and more on the positive, constructive steps you can take.

In business and in life, the better you get at solving problems, the bigger will be the problems you will be given to solve. The bigger and more costly the problems you solve, the more money you will be paid, the more power you will have, and the higher position you will attain. As General Colin Powell said in a Barbara Walters interview, "Leadership is the ability to solve problems."

Your success in your career will be largely determined by your ability to solve the problems that you meet at your level. When you demonstrate that you can solve your current problems, you will be promoted to dealing with problems of greater complexity and importance, just as you get promoted to a higher grade in school when you have passed the exams at your current level.

Resolve to be solution oriented in your approach toward life and work. Be the kind of person that people bring their problems to because you always have good ideas about how to solve them. The more you focus on solutions, the more effectively you think and the better solutions you come up with. You can put your entire life and career on the fast track toward being paid more and promoted faster by becoming an intensely solution-oriented person.

◆

TAKE ACTION NOW!

Ask yourself these questions every day: "What am I trying to do? How am I trying to do it? Could there be a better way?"

What is the limiting factor or constraint that determines how fast you achieve your most important goal or get your most important result? What one problem, if you solved it, would help you the most to move ahead more rapidly in your career?

Write your key problem today at the top of a page in the form of a question. Discipline yourself to write a minimum of twenty answers to this question. Select one of these answers and take action on it immediately. Think in terms of solutions for the rest of your career.

Unlock Your Inborn Creativity

The man who comes up with a means
for doing or producing almost
anything better, faster, or more
economically has his future and his
fortune at his fingertips.

— J. PAUL GETTY

Your ability to generate new ideas and innovations can be more important than any other ability you develop. Many people have changed their entire lives with a single insight that led to a major market breakthrough or to tremendous cost savings. You should always be using your creativity to find faster, cheaper, easier ways to do your job and achieve better results.

The fact is that, based on everything known about learning abilities and multiple intelligences, you are a potential genius! You have more natural intelligence and creativity than you will ever need to achieve all your goals. But your creativity is like a muscle. If you don't use it, you lose it. If you do use your mental abilities, however, they grow stronger. The more you use your mind to generate ideas, the more creative you become and the more and better ideas you come up with to use in every part of your work.

The most successful people in every business are those who are always looking for new and better ideas, new and better ways to achieve the goals of the company. As it happens, everyone is smart and capable in his or her own way. No one is better than you. No one has more natural creativity than you, just as no one has different muscles than you. What really matters is how often and how well you use your creative potential in your life and your work.

To become a more creative person, you can do several things to stimulate ideas. Start by reading books, magazines, and newsletters in your industry. Talk to other people in your field and in other fields. Study different businesses and industries and imagine how their methods of sales, production, or distribution could transfer to your business. Keep looking for ideas, even unusual ideas, that you could adapt to help your company to be more profitable.

There is a direct relationship between creativity and success. The more ideas you come up with to improve the operations of your business, the more you will be paid and the faster you will be promoted. One good idea is all it takes to change the direction of your career.

◆ ────────────────────────

TAKE ACTION NOW!

Unlock your creative powers by continually applying them, like a laser beam, to your work and your personal life. In thinking creatively, the key word is *clarity*. To stimulate more and better ideas, you need absolute clarity in three areas: goals, problems, and questions.

Become absolutely clear about your most intensely desired goals, business and personal. Write them down.

Define the most pressing problems in your life and career. Define them clearly.

Ask pointed questions that force you to think out of the box. And most of all, think on paper to concentrate your mind and trigger your inner genius.

Put People First in Everything

There is no higher religion than human service. To work for the common good is the greatest creed.

— ALBERT SCHWEITZER

In business and personal life, people are everything. Your level of success, your rate of promotion, and the size of your income will be largely determined by the number of people you know and who know and like you. The more that people like and respect you, the more doors they will open for you and the more obstacles they will remove from your path.

The key to becoming a people-oriented person is for you to practice the Golden Rule in everything you do: Treat other people the way you would like them to treat you. Offer to help other people in their work whenever you see an opportunity. Practice being courteous, kind, and considerate when you deal with fellow employees, especially people who work in lesser-paid positions than your own.

The Law of Reciprocity is the major force in human affairs. This law says that we always strive to pay people back for anything they do for us (or to us). This extension of the Law of Sowing and Reaping from the Bible or of Newton's third law of physics says that for every action, there is an equal and opposite reaction. This principle governs most human affairs.

You can implement this law in your career by always looking for ways to help others, both inside and outside your company. Take every opportunity to expand your network of contacts. Join your local business association and attend every meeting and function related to your field. Introduce yourself to other people and find out what they do. Ask good questions and listen carefully to the answers. Look for ways to help others achieve their business goals.

In your work, be a friendly, helpful, and cheerful person. Express gratitude to people on every occasion. Say "thank you" to anyone who does anything for you, either large or small. Go out of your way to compliment people on their traits, possessions, or accomplishments. As Abraham Lincoln said, "Everybody likes a compliment."

Treat each person you work with as if he or she was one of the most valuable customers of the business. Treat your boss, your coworkers, and your staff as if they were all valuable and important people. When you make other people feel important, they will look for every opportunity to make you feel important as well.

When you are genuinely liked and respected by all the people around you, all kinds of opportunities will open up for you to be paid more and promoted faster.

TAKE ACTION NOW!

Make a list of all the important people in your work life, both inside and outside the company. Review this list and think about the kinds of results you would like to enjoy in your relationships with these people.

Think about what you could do for someone that would cause him or her to want to help you or support you. Practice the Law of Sowing and Reaping. Be a "go-giver" rather than a "go-getter." Look for ways to put something into the relationship before you think about getting something out.

Invest in Yourself Continually

Let me look upward into the branches
of the towering oak and know that
it grew great and strong because it
grew slowly and well.

—WILFRED A. PETERSON

Dedicate yourself to lifelong learning. Set yourself apart from the crowd by being the one person in the company who is learning and growing at a faster rate than anyone else. This single decision can give you a personal competitive advantage throughout your career.

The fact is that most of your knowledge and skill today has a half-life of about two and a half years. This means that within five years, most of what you know about your business today will be obsolete or ir-relevant. To survive and thrive in the fast-changing world of tomorrow, you will have to continually up-grade your knowledge and skills at a faster and faster rate. You will have to study and learn aggressively just to stay even, much less to get ahead. As Pat Riley, the basketball coach, said, "If you're not getting better, you're getting worse."

The highest paid 10 percent of Americans read two to three hours each day in their fields just to keep current. They are continually taking in new informa-tion from every possible source. Their minds are like sponges, absorbing newspapers, magazines, books, and key radio and television programs. Reid Buckley wrote in his book *Public Speaking,* "If you are not con-tinually learning and upgrading your knowledge and skills, somewhere someone else is. And when you meet that person, you will lose."

As we move at hyperspeed into the information age, the top people in every business realize that they must stay ahead and on top of the wave of change or they will be bowled over by it. Today, you have a very simple choice. You can be a master of change or you can be a victim of change. There is very little middle ground. Your job is to be a master of change by con-tinually learning to be better and better at whatever you do.

There are three keys to lifelong learning. The first is for you to read at least one hour each day, and more when you can, in your chosen field. Reading is to the mind as exercise is to the body. If you read one hour a day from a good book in your field each day, that will translate into about one book per week. One book per week will equal approximately fifty books per year. Fifty books per year will amount to 500 books over the next ten years. The daily practice of continuously reading in your field will make you one of the best-educated and highest paid people in your business in a very short time.

The second key to continuous learning is for you to listen to audio programs in your car as you drive from place to place. The average car owner sits behind the wheel 500 to 1,000 hours each year. This is the equivalent of three to six months of forty-hour weeks that you spend in your car. According to the University of Southern California, this is equal to one to two full-time university semesters. You can become one of the best-informed people in your field by listening to educational audio programs rather than music in your car.

The third key to continuous learning is for you to take every course and seminar that you can find. The highest paid people I know will actually travel from one side of the country to the other in order to take an intense two- or three-day seminar that can help them in their business activities. A good book, audio program, or seminar can give you ideas and insights that can save you years of hard work.

Become hungry for new knowledge. Seek it everywhere. Soak it up like a sponge. Continuous personal and professional development will unlock more of your potential and open every door for you. Nothing can help you to get paid more and promoted faster than becoming one of the most knowledgeable and competent people in your field, and continuous learning is the key.

TAKE ACTION NOW!

Begin a daily reading program immediately. Resolve to go to bed early and get up two hours before you have to leave for work. Invest the first hour, the "Golden Hour," in yourself, in your mind. This commitment to reading something educational, inspirational, or motivational will set the tone for the rest of the day and will eventually change your life.

Turn your car into a "university on wheels." Never let your car move without an educational audio program playing. Since audio programs often contain the best ideas of several books, you can save yourself an enormous amount of time and money by simply turning driving time into learning time.

Commit to Excellence

Your success in life will be determined
more by the depth of your commitment
to excellence than by any other factor,
no matter what your chosen field.

—Vince Lombardi

Resolve to be the very best at what you do. Resolve
today to join the top 10 percent of people in your
field. Look around you at the best people and remember that they all started at the bottom. If they
could do it, so can you. No one is smarter than you
and no one is better than you. If someone is ahead of
you today, it is because he or she is doing something
differently from you. And whatever anyone else has
accomplished, within reason, you can accomplish as
well, if you just learn how.

The starting point of becoming one of the best people in your field is for you to identify your *key result*

areas at work. These are the skill areas where you absolutely, positively have to do an excellent job in order to get the results by which your success at work is judged by your boss.

A job seldom has more than five to seven key result areas. Your ability to perform at an excellent level in each of these areas is the key determinant of how well you perform overall. These results or outputs determine how much you are paid and how fast you are promoted.

Once you have identified your key result areas, ask yourself this question: *"What one skill, if I developed and did it in an excellent fashion, would have the greatest positive impact on my career?"*

This is one of the most important questions you will ever ask and answer throughout your working life. If you do not know which one skill can help you the most at this time, go to your boss and ask him or her for advice. Ask your coworkers. Ask your spouse. But whatever it takes, you absolutely must determine the one skill that can help you the most. You must then dedicate yourself to improving in this area as if your future depended on it—because it does.

Once you are clear about the one skill that can help you the most, set the acquisition of this skill as a goal. Write it down, make a plan, and then work on getting better in this area every single day. The daily exercise of focusing on improvement in your key result areas, one at a time, is so powerful that this commitment alone can change your entire life.

Quality work is everything. Resolve today to become absolutely excellent at what you do. Commit to doing your job the very best way possible. Set excellent performance as your standard and never compromise it for the rest of your career.

◆

TAKE ACTION NOW!

Your life only gets better when you get better. Make a list of every task you perform, every key result you are expected to get for your company. Examine your list, discuss it with others, and then identify the one skill that if you did it extremely well, would have the most positive impact on your career.

Develop standards of performance, measurements for your key result areas. "What gets measured gets done." Determine the numbers you will use to measure how well you are doing in each part of your work. Compare your performance with your standards regularly to track your progress. Continually strive to improve.

Concentrate on the Customer

No man has ever risen to the real stature
of spiritual manhood until he has found
that it is finer to serve somebody else
than it is to serve himself.

—Woodrow Wilson

We have entered the "age of the customer." We know today that the real purpose of a business is to create and keep customers. To achieve any level of business success, customers must become the central focus of every activity. Profits in a business are the result of creating and keeping customers in a sufficient number and at a reasonable cost.

Customers pay all salaries and wages. Customers determine the success or failure of companies and of everyone in the company. Sam Walton, the founder of Wal-Mart, once said, "We all have one boss, the customer, and he can fire us at any time by simply deciding to shop somewhere else."

Who are your customers, both internal and external? Who are your key customers, the people whose decisions most determine success or failure for you and for your company?

The definition of a customer is "someone who depends on you for the satisfaction of his or her needs or someone upon whom you depend for the satisfaction of your needs."

By this definition, your boss is your customer. Your coworkers are your customers. Your staff are your customers. And of course, the people who buy your products and services are your customers. Everyone is dependent on someone else for something. Everyone is someone's customer.

Your success in your life and your career will be totally determined by how well you serve and satisfy the customers in your life. And the more and the better you satisfy your customers, the more customers you will be given to satisfy.

Customer satisfaction has four levels. Where you stand today relative to these levels largely determines how valuable and important you are to your customers and to your organization.

The first level of customer satisfaction is simply *meeting* customer expectations. This is the minimum requirement for business survival. If all you do is the job you were hired to do or work exactly the hours you were hired to work, your present may be satisfactory but your future is not promising.

The next level of satisfaction is where you *exceed* your customers' expectations. You actually go beyond what customers thought they were going to get. This level will keep you in business for a while, until your competitors offer the same or more to lure your customers away. And they will, faster than you can imagine.

The next higher level of customer satisfaction is when you *delight* your customers. You add something to your offering that is completely unexpected and very much appreciated. This can be as simple as phoning a customer after a purchase to be sure that he or she is satisfied or to answer any questions he or she might have. In your work, you delight your boss by showing extra initiative and doing something to help the company that is a complete surprise.

The highest level of all is the fourth, where you *amaze* your customers. You do something that is so far beyond their expectations that they want to buy from you again and tell all their friends about their experience.

The creator of Post-it Notes at 3M Corporation put together a team of specialists who worked on their own time to develop the product. Their eventual success and the billion-dollar market they created became the stuff of legend in the business world.

Every single day, you should be looking for ways to meet expectations, exceed expectations, and both delight and amaze the people who depend upon you at work. Your ability to serve and satisfy your particular customers better than anyone else will get you paid more and promoted faster than almost anything else you can do.

◆

TAKE ACTION NOW!

Identify your most important customers, both inside and outside your business. Remember, your boss, your colleagues, your coworkers, and your staff members are all customers as well.

Make a plan to increase the quality and quantity of your service to them so that they will be more willing to help and support you in doing your job and achieving your goals.

Identify your most important customers outside your firm, both the people who buy what you sell and also the people whose cooperation you require to serve them well. Determine what you could do to improve these relationships. Take action on your decision today.

Focus on the Bottom Line

Men who accomplish great things
in the industrial world are those
who have faith in the money producing
power of their ideas.

—CHARLES FILLMORE

Profit orientation is the key to your future. Intense bottom-line focus is the key to growth, success, and rapid promotion. The very best people in every organization are thinking constantly about what they can do to increase the profitability of their companies. The greater impact your work has on net cash flow, the more important you become and the more you will be paid.

Only two basic ways exist to increase profitability in your company. The first is to increase revenues, by selling more of your existing products and services or by developing new products and services that can be sold to more customers.

The second way to increase profitability is to reduce the costs of providing your products and services to your current customers. The very best profit improvement strategy is for you to continually look for ways to increase sales and revenues while at the same time reduce the costs of delivering those products and services.

Each day you should seek ways to reorganize, restructure, and reengineer your work so that you can do your job faster and at a lower cost than before. Squeeze out every extra penny of expense. Examine every single cost to see if it cannot be reduced. Look at every activity to see if it cannot be simplified, downsized, or even eliminated to reduce time and expenditure in getting the desired result.

The most valuable and appreciated people in any organization are those who are the most concerned with the overall profitability of the company. They treat every economic activity of the company as if it affected them personally. They treat the company's money as if it were their own. They take full responsibility for the results of the business.

When you become a key player in increasing profitability in some way, you come immediately to the attention of the people who can most help you in your career. Your ability to boost profitability by increasing revenues or cutting costs is one of the very fastest ways for you to get paid more and promoted faster.

TAKE ACTION NOW!

Begin today to treat your company as if it belonged to you and every single dollar either came out of your pocket or went into your pocket. Treat every expense as if it affected you personally. Find at least one way today to reduce costs or simplify activities.

The lifeblood of a business is sales and cash flow. Study your business closely and determine how you could increase sales or cash flow in some way. One good idea could change your career.

Develop Positive Personal Power

Today, knowledge has power. It controls access to opportunity and advancement.

—PETER DRUCKER

Power is a very real and important part of organizational and business life. Your ability to acquire and use power in your career is essential to your long-term success.

"Power," in its simplest sense, means influence over people and resources. To have power means that you have the ability to determine what people do and how money is spent. With power, you can make decisions or alter decisions that have been made by others. You can decide what actions will be taken, or you can stop things from being done.

Two kinds of power exist in a company: positive power and negative power. Positive power is what you demonstrate when you use your strengths to help the organization achieve more of its goals faster and cheaper. Negative power is demonstrated when a person uses position or influence to improve himself or himself at the expense of other people or the organization.

You can develop three forms of positive power. The first is called "expert power." Expert power arises when you become excellent at getting a result that is important to your company. Because of your ability to contribute value, people look up to you and respect you for the positive difference you make in the organization.

The second form of power is called "personality power." You acquire this form of power when you are liked and respected by others, when you are popular and personable. Personality power arises when people like you and want you to be successful. Every organization has people with great attitudes who have tremendous influence even though they may not be in key positions. This form of power is based on a positive, constructive attitude more than anything else.

The third kind of power you can develop is "position power." This power comes with a job title and includes the authority to hire and fire people and to reward or punish particular behaviors. Every title or position has this power attached to it.

In your company and your career, as you develop expert power and personality power, which are very much under your control, you will be given position power. The people above you and around you will want you to be promoted because you have demonstrated that the more influence you have, the more and better results you can get for the company.

The more you acquire and use your power in a positive and constructive way, the more power you will attract to you. More people around you will support you and help you. The people above you will give you more resources and greater responsibilities. You will be more respected and esteemed by others. You will definitely be paid more and promoted faster.

◆

TAKE ACTION NOW!

Leadership has been defined as the ability to get followers. Use the Law of Indirect Effort to develop power and influence in your organization by always looking for ways to help the company achieve its most important goals. Look for ways to help other people succeed in their jobs.

Develop positive power: when you use your influence and ability for the good of the company and of the people who work there, others will want you to succeed and be promoted.

Get the Job Done Fast

Always bear in mind that your own
resolution to succeed is more important
than any other one thing.

—ABRAHAM LINCOLN

Action orientation is the most outwardly identifiable quality of a high performing man or woman. Such a person takes initiative and develops a sense of urgency. He or she is constantly in motion. He or she is always doing something that is moving the company toward the achievement of its most important goals, and doing it quickly.

Develop a bias for action. Develop a fast tempo in everything you do. Decide what needs to be done and then get on with it. Don't procrastinate or delay.

The good news is that the faster you move, the more you get done. The more you get done, the more experience you get and the more competent you become. The faster you move, the more energy you have. The faster you move, the smarter and more creative you become. The faster you move, the more valuable you become to your company and to everyone around you.

Only about 2 percent of people in our society have a sense of urgency. These are the people who eventually rise to the top of their organizations. When you develop a reputation for speed and dependability in everything you do, you attract to yourself more and more opportunities to do more and more things of greater and greater importance.

Of course, doing things quickly does not mean that you should sacrifice quality. Always do your work in an excellent fashion. But do it as fast as you can. And the more important it is to the future of the company, the sooner you should start and complete it. An average person with an average background who reacts quickly and moves fast will eventually run circles around a genius who only does a job when he or she gets around to it.

One of your key goals at work should be to develop the reputation for being the person whom people give a job to if they want it done fast. This reputation for speed and dependability will open every door for you. It will get you paid more and promoted faster than almost anything else you can possibly do.

TAKE ACTION NOW!

Begin each day by making a list of everything you have to do that day. Organize your
list by priority by putting an A, B, or C next
to each task. An A task is very important, a
B task is of medium importance, and a C
task is not really important at all.

Then organize your "A" tasks by priority
by writing A-1, A-2, A-3, and so on next to
each one. Once you have determined your
"A-1" task, the most important single thing
you can do, start on it immediately. Do it
now. This habit of moving fast on your top
task will enable you to get more important
tasks completed than any other habit you
can develop.

Conclusion:
Moving onto the Fast
Track in Your Career

L et me conclude this book by repeating a key point. You are in charge of your career and your future. No one else cares as much as you do. No one else will make the key decisions for you. You are responsible. And there are no limits to what you can accomplish with your virtually unlimited variety of talents and abilities.

This is one of the very best times in all of human history to be alive. There are more opportunities for you to get paid more and promoted faster today than have ever before existed. You can make more progress in a few years today than your parents or grandparents might have been able to make in a lifetime. Your job is to do everything you can to participate fully in this "Golden Age" by practicing these twenty-one great ideas for the rest of your career.

Here they are, once more:

1. **Decide exactly what you want.** You can't hit a target you can't see. Define your ideal job and never stop striving until you get it.

2. **Select the Right Company.** Do your homework and be sure you are committing yourself to a company where you can make the greatest progress.

3. **Choose the Right Boss.** Be sure that you like, respect, and feel that you can perform at your best for this boss.

4. **Develop a Positive Attitude.** Look for the good in every situation and dedicate yourself to being the kind of person that others want to work with and help succeed.

5. **Create a Successful Image.** Take the time to dress, groom, and look like a winner in all your work activities.

6. **Start Earlier, Work Harder, and Stay Later.** Always look for ways to go the extra mile, to do more than you're paid for.

7. **Push to the Front.** Dedicate yourself to making the most valuable contribution you possibly can.

8. **Ask for What You Want.** Speak out clearly and ask for more responsibility, more opportunities, and more money.

9. **Guard Your Integrity as a Sacred Thing.** Be honest, straightforward, and truthful in all your interactions with others.

10. **Think about the Future.** Continually look for ways to improve your company and your work in the weeks and months ahead.

11. **Focus on Your Goals.** Determine exactly what you want to achieve, and work on your major goals every single day.

12. **Concentrate on Results.** Focus your mental and physical energies on getting the most important results in your job.

13. **Be a Problem Solver.** Continually look for better, faster, cheaper ways to solve the problems facing your company and your boss.

14. **Unlock Your Inborn Creativity.** Practice tapping into your mind to come up with ideas to help your company get results faster, cheaper, and easier than ever before.

15. **Put People First in Everything.** Look for ways to help your boss and others make their greatest contributions to the company.

16. **Invest in Yourself Continually.** Read, study, attend seminars, and listen to audio programs every single day to increase your knowledge and skills.

17. **Commit to Excellence.** Resolve to become very good at doing those things that are really important to your company and to your customers.

18. **Concentrate on the Customer.** Place the needs and well-being of your customers at the center of all decision making.

19. **Focus on the Bottom Line.** Treat every source of revenue and expense as if it were your own money and always look for ways to improve the financial results of your company.

20. **Develop Positive Personal Power.** Resolve to become the kind of person with the expertise and the personality to get ever greater results for your organization.

21. **Get the Job Done Fast.** Develop a reputation for being the person who gets results faster and more dependably than anyone else.

Today, the primary sources of wealth are talent and ability, knowledge and ideas. Money and resources flow to the men and women who demonstrate that they can get the job done quickly and well.

When you begin to practice these twenty-one great ways to get paid more and promoted faster, you will put your career onto the fast track. You will move ahead more rapidly than anyone else around you. You will move upward and onward and you will make your life and career into something truly extraordinary. There are no limits. Take action today!

Learning Resources of
Brian Tracy International

BRIAN TRACY AUDIO LEARNING PROGRAMS

	AUDIO	CD
❖ **Psychology of Achievement** (7 hours) The most popular program on success and achievement in the world.	$65.00	$70.00
❖ **Psychology of Success** (7 hours) The 10 principles of peak performance practiced by all high achievers.	$65.00	$70.00
❖ **Psychology of Selling** (7 hours) The most powerful, practical, professional selling program in the world today.	$75.00	$80.00
❖ **How to Master Your Time** (7 hours) More than 500 key ideas for time management in a proven system that brings about immediate results. Save 2 hours every day.	$65.00	$70.00
❖ **Million-Dollar Habits** (7 hours) The specific habits and behaviors practiced by high earners and self-made millionaires. Double and triple your income.	$65.00	$70.00
❖ **How Leaders Lead** (7 hours) With Ken Blanchard. How to manage, motivate, inspire, and lead a winning team.	$65.00	
❖ **Advanced Selling Techniques** (7 hours) The most complete advanced selling program for top professionals in the world.	$75.00	$80.00
❖ **Master Strategies for High Achievement** (7 hours) More than 150 of the key strategies practiced by the most successful people--in every area of life.	$65.00	$70.00

	AUDIO	CD
❖ **Accelerated Learning Techniques** (7 hours) How to learn faster, remember more, unlock the power of your mind for maximum performance.	$65.00	$70.00
❖ **Thinking Big** (7 hours) How to dream big dreams, build self-confidence, set goals, develop the mind-set of successful people.	$65.00	$70.00
❖ **The Luck Factor** (7 hours) More than 60 proven strategies to increase the likelihood that you will be the right person at the right place at the right time.	$65.00	$70.00
❖ **Breaking the Success Barrier** (7 hours) The 12 most powerful thinking tools ever discovered enable you to overcome any obstacle, achieve any goal.	$65.00	$70.00

❖ SPECIAL OFFER ❖

Any 1 program—$65 • 2–3 programs—$60 each

4–5 programs—$55 each • Any 6 programs—$295

Any 10 programs—$450

To order one or more of these programs, phone 800/542-4252, visit our Web site at www.briantracy.com, or write to Brian Tracy International, 462 Stevens Avenue, Suite 202, Solana Beach, CA 92075. Fax: 858/481-2445.

Unconditionally guaranteed for one full year or your money back!

If you are not delighted with these learning programs, return the materials for a complete refund any time in the year following the date of purchase.

BRIAN TRACY
SPEAKER · AUTHOR · TRAINER

Brian Tracy addresses more than 250,000 people each year in talks and seminars, from keynote addresses to sessions three to four days in length.

His topics include

- High Performance Leadership for the 21st Century
- Maximizing Personal Performance
- Advanced Selling Skills and Strategies

For more information, visit www.briantracy.com, where you can also get a free subscription to one or more of Brian's helpful newsletters on Personal Success, Time Management, and Financial Mastery.

To book Brian as a speaker, contact

Brian Tracy International
462 Stevens Avenue, Suite 202
Solana Beach, CA 92075
Phone 858-481-2977
Fax 858-481-2445
www.briantracy.com

The 100 Absolutely Unbreakable Laws of Business Success

Why are some people more successful in business than others? Why do some businesses flourish where others fail? Renowned business speaker and author Brian Tracy has discovered the answers to these profoundly puzzling questions. In this eye-opening practical guide, he presents a set of principles, or "universal laws," that lie behind the success of businesspeople everywhere. *The 100 Absolutely Unbreakable Laws of Business Success* will teach you how to • attract and keep better people • produce and sell more and better products and services • control costs more intelligently • expand and grow more predictably • increase your profits, and much more.

Hardcover, 300 pages, ISBN 1-57675-107-4, Item #51074, $24.95
Audiocassette, 4 cassettes/6 hours, ISBN 1-57675-121-X, Item #5121X, $25.00

The 21 Success Secrets of Self-Made Millionaires
How to Achieve Financial Independence Faster and Easier Than You Ever Thought Possible

Learn how ordinary people achieve extraordinary financial results! This exciting book from best-selling author Brian Tracy provides a practical step-by-step formula for becoming a millionaire—starting from wherever you are today. You'll learn how to set goals, make plans, and organize yourself to get more of what you really want in life.

Hardcover, 96 pages, ISBN 1-58376-205-1, Item #62051, $19.95
Audiocassette, 1 cassette/70 minutes, ISBN 1-57675-122-8, Item #51228, $14.95

Available at your favorite bookstore or e-store or from Berrett-Koehler Publishers at www.bkconnection.com or (800) 929-2929.

Index

About the Author

BRIAN TRACY is one of the top professional speakers and trainers in the world today. He addresses more than 250,000 men and women each year on the subjects of leadership, strategy, sales, and personal and business success.

Brian is an avid student of business, psychology, management, sales, history, economics, politics, metaphysics, and religion. He brings a unique blend of humor, insight, information, and inspiration to the more than 100 talks and seminars he conducts worldwide each year.

Brian believes that each person has extraordinary untapped potential that he or she can learn to access and, in so doing, accomplish more in a few years than the average person does in a lifetime.

Brian Tracy is the chairman of Brian Tracy International, a human resource development company headquartered in Solana Beach, California. He has written sixteen books and produced more than 300 audio and video training programs. His materials have been translated into twenty languages and are used in thirty-eight countries.

Brian lives with his wife, Barbara, and their four children in Solana Beach, California. He is active in community affairs and serves as a consultant to several nonprofit organizations. This book is a summary of the most important principles for career success that he has discovered in thirty years of hard work and experience.